Hold Nothing Back!

Overcome your fears and
achieve your dreams.

Hold Nothing Back!

Overcome your fears and
achieve your dreams.

by Mike Jones

Printed in the United States of America.

ISBN: 1-888237-53-8

Dedicated

Michael　　　　*Matthew*　　　　*Christian*　　　　*Jeremy*

These four handsome young men are the reason I chose
to Hold Nothing Back in my life.

Table of Contents

Acknowledgements

D*i*SCOVER
Leadership Training

Each person on my team at Discover Leadership Training has joined me heart, body, and soul to propel individuals, teams, and companies to the pinnacle of achievement and fulfillment. Our team continues to grow and I want to thank Diana Nicholson, Karol Hartzell, Shelli Alaniz, Mary Breitigam and Melanie Manning for their commitment to me and to our shared purpose of changing lives.

—*The Author*

Introduction

Those who come to Discover Leadership Training hope our time together will give them two important things: hope and anchors. If I asked them to rate their level of satisfaction with their lives when they walk in the door, many of them would honestly say, "Oh, pretty good," or "OK, I guess." But when they walk out, the vast majority of them have a fresh, new sense of purpose. Their convictions are sharpened, and they believe—really believe—that their lives can be something special! And they have clear strategies to help them take steps to reach the outcomes they have defined.

I want this book to provide hope and anchors for you, too. The principles and stories in these pages are designed to show you that—no matter how difficult your life has been and no matter how many obstacles you face—you can take incredible steps toward a rich, rewarding life. But that doesn't happen by magic. Change happens when we clearly see our choices and muster the courage to make them. This book also provides anchors for the process of change, learning to think with positive instead of negative assumptions, overcoming your fears, and taking strong bold steps to reach the outcomes you want to reach.

But I want to warn you. This is not a collection of warm fuzzies. The steps to a meaningful, successful life include tough decisions and tenacity to keep going, as well as times of joyful exhilaration.

If you long for your life to be richer and more rewarding, if you want your relationships to be deeper and stronger, if you hope to make your life count in the lives of others, keep reading. This book is for you.

Focus on Outcomes

Beginnings and Endings

In Steven Covey's best seller, *7 Habits of Highly Effective People*, one of his maxims is, "Begin with the end in mind." Most of us don't do that. We begin with little thought of what we want the outcome to be. Without a clearly defined outcome, we have no way to measure success . . . or even to measure steps of progress! We work hard, but our efforts are scattered, and we settle for mediocrity. The only way to make sure you make the right choices when you get to a point of decision is to clearly define your desired outcome and remain focused on it. That's beginning with the end in mind. Unless you set an outcome you can not identify if you are holding back or not.

To put a handle on the process of defining desired outcomes, I use the acronym, WAYFO? It means: *What are you focused on?* It is a simple, effective question to change your focus to change your results. It clarifies the outcome you want to achieve, focuses your attention, and directs your time and energies. Where your attention goes, your energy flows. Your energy and action follow your thoughts. What gets your attention gets you. I guarantee it.

So, what is your desired outcome?

A lady once told me her outcome was to be a better mother. That's wonderful, but it's too broad to be an effective outcome. I said, "Let's break it down into something measurable." Then I asked her, "What is your description of a good mother? What does a good mother do to ensure her family is strong and healthy?"

One of her answers to those questions was to carve out quality time for the family to communicate with each other. Here's the desired outcome she established. She determined: "I will make sure we eat at home five out of seven nights a week." That gave her a specific focus, something for which she could be accountable. To create this outcome, her action plan for the first week was to plan a simple menu that everyone would enjoy, spend some time cooking, involve others in the process, and eat at home.

One of the daily outcomes I want to accomplish is running. When I go to bed at night, I set the alarm clock for 3:30 a.m. so I can be out in the park by 4:00 a.m.

The night before, I also set my outcome for how many miles I'll run. Regardless of how I feel that morning, I'm committed, and I'm going to do what I said I would do, no holding back. Some mornings, I'm really tired. If I hadn't set that outcome, I don't think I'd drag myself out of bed that early. Most likely, I'd find some excuses (cleverly disguised as good reasons) to turn over and go back to sleep. But once the outcome is set the night before, I stick with it. I may be exhausted when I'm finished running. However, at the very least, I feel good about keeping my commitment.

I train myself to live that way. I train myself to live in the moment and give heart, body, and soul to every thing I do. It takes discipline.

Clear Outcomes and the Wind

In *Change Your Mind—Change Your World*, I described the difference between "the flag" and "the wind." People who are flags are passive, blown by outside influences. They live their lives holding back. But those who are the wind take initiative and chart their own course. They make a difference! If you never set desired outcomes, you are the flag. You have no drive and no direction, and no one can count on you because you are inconsistent. The circumstances of the moment and the desires of others determine your reactions. Every time the wind blows, your energy and focus do whatever those outside forces dictate. It may be easier to let others determine the course of your life, but it's a frustrating, empty way to live.

Remember, energy and action follow thought. If you aren't focused on clearly defined outcomes, your energy and action drift with the prevailing winds. It may take you in the direction you want to go one minute, but in the opposite direction the next. **Stop being a flag. Be the wind!**

When you have clear, attainable outcomes, you'll make decisions each moment to take steps toward those ends. Defining your desired outcomes creates new behaviors and new possibilities.

In the same book, I described how all of us have a set of presuppositions, perspectives, and beliefs that determine how we analyze each moment and make each choice. This set of concepts is a person's mental "map." When we don't define clear outcomes, we fall prey to all the fears and confusion on our distorted maps. We have tunnel vision, seeing only the same old possibilities (or impossibilities!), directed by the same old fears and drives. As a result we hold back. Clarifying the outcomes we really want, however, broadens our vision, opens new possibilities, instills confidence, and gives us courage to take steps we've never taken before. When we are outcome-focused, we hold nothing back, we keep learning, and we'll do everything in our power to accomplish our purpose.

Dream Big!

To get the right conversation going in your head—and begin to change your map—start with one big vision for your life. Then focus on the specific outcomes you want in every area: your professional career, family, friends, fun, health, finances, and every other important area of your life. Your future is

Dreams give you energy. They give you a reason to get up each morning, and they provide the tenacity to keep going when things get tough.

a blank canvas. You can design it by determining the outcomes you want and making the choices that are in line with each one.

Thinking big is good. Expand your vision and your expectations. Dream about making a difference—a big difference!—in others' lives. Dreams give you energy. They give you a reason to get up each morning, and they provide the tenacity to keep going when things get tough. Thinking big changes your map (your assumptions, hopes, and fears), and gives clear direction to your choices.

Years ago, I was involved in "Soul Patrol," a very popular and successful program to teach values to high school students. I rode the wave of success, and it was fulfilling . . . up to a point. That work, though, was something that happened to me. It wasn't something I designed myself. Discover Leadership Training is the dream God gave me to touch each and every person on the globe. Yes, that's right, the entire world! Each of us has an impact on five to five thousand people, so as Discover touches one life, the ripple effect impacts dozens, hundreds, and even thousands of others, who then impact even more. In the last few years, we've touched men and women from Asia and the Pacific Rim, Australia, Europe, Africa, and Latin America. The dream is happening!

One of my favorite times in our training is toward the end when people communicate the benefits they've received. Those who come from foreign lands and speak English as a second language often have difficulty finding the right words. They want to pour out their hearts, but the words just don't come, so we invite them to share their hearts in their own languages. In most cases, I don't have a clue what they are saying, but the passion and richness of their messages are unmistakable! All of us get chills as we see and hear these men and women communicate the life-changing insights and their commitments to never be the same.

I get up every morning with a clear strategy to achieve that colossal dream, and I can't wait to get going! Nothing is going to stop us. I will hold nothing back regarding my vision to create the most sought after and recognized leadership program on the planet. My team at Discover Leadership Training knows that "Obstacles" aren't obstacles at all. They are only stepping stones to help us learn and grow so we become even more effective. With the dream to have an impact on the planet, and with the sights and sounds of people's lives being changed forever, I am energized to fulfill my calling and achieve that dream. Every day, my team and I work hard to expand our impact and fine-tune our strategy so we can touch as many as possible as powerfully as possible.

Check the conversation you are having in your head each day. Are you having the right one? Are you talking to yourself about big dreams that give you energy and life?

Dreaming big is a great start, but then you begin to refine that vision. If it's too broad, it probably won't be accomplished. Refining your outcomes makes the individual choice points even clearer.

Check the conversation you are having in your head each day. Are you having the right one? Are you talking to yourself about big dreams that give you energy and life? Or do you continually pummel yourself for being such a failure? Are your thoughts dominated by your fears, and do you talk to yourself about avoiding risk at all costs? Do you daydream about being miraculously rescued out of your dull, empty experience and given a life of wealth and comfort (maybe by winning the lottery)? Develop the habit and the skill of right thinking. **Have conversations with yourself that focus on hope, courage, and the impact you want to have in this life.** You are far more likely to achieve your dreams if you have the right conversations, use optimistic words, and focus on the right things. Will there be barriers? Of course! Stop and picture the benefits on the other side of any barrier. Think positively, because energy and action follow thought.

A negative map is self-defeating . . . and it's entirely predictable. You have probably seen the same scenario a thousand times. I've watched people, especially women, get out of bad relationships, and they swear they'll never end up with anyone like that again! They're absolutely determined, but for some reason, they fall into the same trap again. They go to a party and find 99 wonderful, respectful, honorable people. But the 100th person is just like the one recently dumped. Because they have such clearly formed assumptions in their maps, they are drawn to that loser like a magnet! They meet, they talk, and soon they are in a serious relationship. Six months later, they are victims again.

A map is an incredibly powerful piece of directional equipment. Our assumptions about what is good and right seem very clear, but they may be very wrong! It's absolutely essential that we step back, analyze our maps, and begin to make major changes in some areas. It's not enough to say, "I don't want this or that." We also need to determine, "This is what I want now!" If we only want to avoid trouble, we'll probably find trouble again soon. We need to focus on achieving the positive, not just trying to avoid the negative. The benefit of a dream, a vision, a clearly defined outcome is to redraw our maps and set a new course for our lives.

Conversations with Yourself about Your Career

Many people are unhappy with their careers. Their internal conversation says, "I hate my job!" That may be an accurate feeling, but it doesn't take you where you want to go. It is a focus on what you "don't" want. That creates an attitude of holding back. Instead of locking your sights on the negative, focus on the positive aspects of your work. Tell yourself, "I'll make this job work for me," or "I'll get a better job." You'll be amazed how changing the conversation you are having with yourself gets you moving in the right direction.

Be specific and positive about the outcomes you want to achieve. If you stay focused on the negatives, you'll feel like a victim and remain passive. You will hold back, you'll be a flag, and drift from job to job, never happy, seldom effective, and usually confused. Ask yourself, "Why do I want a better job? What is this one not producing for me?" Know what you're looking for. Identify what you want and need in your employment, then make a solid determination: "This is what I will do, and this is why." When you identify specific, positive outcomes, you commit your energy to reach them. You will hold nothing back.

Many people are in jobs they aren't crazy about, but those jobs provide income for them to take care of their families. Should they stay there? That's a good question.

No job is perfect. Seek to understand the benefits

of your job and the positive reasons to stay. You can be excited about the lifestyle you are providing for your family, enough disposable income so you can travel together, and the funds to send your children to college. Those are significant benefits, and they may be worth putting up with some headaches at work.

If the lines on your map direct you in a negative direction, you'll focus on everything you hate about your job: your dumb boss, boring assignments, imbeciles at the corporate office, long hours, and a host of other hassles. This kind of thinking is sure to put you into a funk!

WAYFO? What are you focused on? You can target your mental energies on the things you don't like about the job, or you can focus on the positives. Make a choice. Take time to write down the benefits of your work, and think about what your life would be like without those

After a few days or a few weeks of being thankful for the benefits of your job, your whole attitude will change.

benefits. Let those positive concepts steep in your mind for a while. When you find yourself going down the wrong road on the map of your negative assumptions, stop and go in a different direction. If you need to rivet these positive thoughts in your mind, write them down and keep the paper in your pocket or purse so you can look at them whenever you need to.

After a few days or a few weeks of being thankful for the benefits of your job, your whole attitude will change. You'll find yourself far happier at work, and you'll spend your mental energies being effective and thankful instead of griping and avoiding tasks.

A person's focus is a function of their attitude. I know plenty of people who have lost their jobs. For some, the mindset is, "Woe is me! The economy is bad, and I'll never get another job like the one I had." He holds back and does not give every thing he has to get what he wants. Their attitude is negative, so their thoughts focus on negative outcomes. But in the same situation, a positive attitude would be stated as, "I'll do whatever it takes to get a job. In fact, I'm going to get a *better* job than I've ever had before!" That attitude rivets the person's mind and heart on possibilities, not problems. She holds nothing back in her commitment to get what she wants. Understand that you can not have an attachment to the outcome—you have no control over how it turns out, however, you do control your choice to hold back or to go for it heart, body and soul.

Of these two attitudes, which one do you think is more likely to get a great new job? An optimistic person may take it on the chin, but he gets up and gets back in the game. The experience of overcoming obstacles helps redraw his map. Every victory like this builds confidence to take the next risk, which will lead to the next victory.

Defining Your Outcomes Clarifies Your Choices

Here's a very specific, simple example of focusing on the outcome you want. Imagine that you've been running a little short on cash, but you determine you'll start saving $10 a week. Where is that $10 going to come from? What are you going to do differently so you can save that money? After all, you didn't save any money when times were better. How in the world can you save any now? To accomplish this outcome, you have to change your approach, which will change the results you produce.

Eating lunch out every day has been draining your cash, so you develop a new plan. You'll make your lunch and take it to work.

On the third day of your plan, you're running late for work. Do you blow off your plan and buy a burger for lunch, or do you stick with your plan and maintain the integrity of your outcome, even if you may run late?

This is where it gets tough because you have to stay focused on the outcome you have set. When you stay focused and are true to your outcome, new behaviors and new possibilities arise.

For instance, if you see that you're regularly running late, consider asking your spouse or your child to make your lunch for you in return for a special reward at the end of the week. On the other hand, you may decide to get more organized in the evenings, making your lunch and getting your morning coffee ready to make with the push of a button. One change triggers another change. When those changes are for the better, everyone wins. You begin to think more creatively, and opportunities that you never knew existed show up on your radar screen.

The most significant rule of thumb for setting a desired outcome is that it has to have substance. Please don't tell me your outcome is that you "just want to be happy!" That's not an outcome because it has no substance, and it isn't measurable. Define what being happy means to you, establish specific outcomes you want to reach, and then make the choices that will result in reaching them. Don't remain passive and hope others will come to your rescue to make you happy. You are the stakeholder in making each individual outcome happen. Grab the responsibility, and don't let go.

Overcome Resistance

You don't have control over whether or not the sun will shine . . . or whether other people will treat you the way you want to be treated. If you have to look to pleasant circumstances and kind people for happiness, you may not find it. **True happiness is contentment that's found in the core of our souls, not at the mercy of situations or people.** We can decide before any event

> **The choices that make you happy are those that are consistent with your dreams and your desired outcomes.**

or circumstance how we will react or respond to it. Happiness is then a choice, more importantly, it's your choice.

The choices that make you happy are those that are consistent with your dreams and your desired outcomes. Your choices are determined by how clearly you've identified those outcomes, not on others "coming through" for you.

Are others' attitudes and actions important in us fulfilling our dreams? Others' affirmation and assistance are *nice*, but they're not *necessary*. If you are committed to whatever it takes to reach your outcomes, it doesn't matter what others do or say. Sure, it would be great if they help you and appreciate you, but your outcomes and your happiness aren't dependent on them. Commit your heart, body, and soul to fulfill your dreams. Don't let anything or anyone stop you. Hold nothing back.

The way we define our outcomes clarifies our choices. Clear choices relieve a lot of stress because they show us what is right or wrong. A decision is right for you when it's in alignment with the outcome you have defined. You may sometimes look at other people and wonder why in the world they made certain choices because you would never have done that! Their choice would be wrong for you because the outcome you want to achieve is different from theirs. But don't be judgmental. Another person's choice might be absolutely right for her because it's in exact alignment with her outcome. Each person is responsible for defining his own outcomes and for the responsibility to reach them.

Let me put a warning label right here. Sometimes we set our outcomes so high that they are unattainable. When we don't achieve them, we run the risk of feeling terribly discouraged. Setting outcomes is a learned skill. All of us experience trial and error as we learn this crucial skill, so give yourself a little room to learn and grow. Don't get too attached to a particular outcome. Hold it loosely, and realize that you may need to make an adjustment or two along the way.

There are many factors over which you have no control. The only factor you have 100% control over is your responsibility to set clear outcomes and follow through to achieve them. Don't let failure take you back to your old, negative map! Don't call yourself ugly names, and don't believe you are a colossal flop. Let each failure be a stepping stone to insight

Fail fast, fail often, and fail forward. The only thing that matters is to learn from your failures, and then you can use that experience to move forward to reach the outcomes you want.

and growth. Again, a positive attitude makes all the difference.

Failure Can Be a Friend

Failure is a precursor for ultimate success. Use it as a learning opportunity. With each experience of success or failure, you learn a little more about what works, what doesn't, and how to be more focused the next time. You can begin again, wiser and smarter. Thomas

Edison said, "The fastest way to succeed is to double your failure rate." Now, that's a positive attitude!

My advice is: Fail fast, fail often, and fail forward. The only thing that matters is to learn from your failures, and then you can use that experience to move forward to reach the outcomes you want.

Failure is not the end of the world. In fact, it may be the beginning of a new day for you! Failure gets our attention, sharpens our insights, and deepens our convictions—if we have a positive, hopeful attitude about it. Failure forces us to analyze our thinking and our assumptions, and it invites us to adjust our maps so we can be 100% focused on the outcomes we long for. We need to hold ourselves accountable for how we respond to failure. Don't grovel in self-pity. Instead, refuse to give up. Every failure is another chance for creating and re-creating good things in our lives.

Be Open and Flexible

Sometimes, success looks much different than we originally envisioned. The process of moving toward the outcome step by step gives us plenty of opportunity to reflect on our dreams—and redefine both the dream and the process of achieving it. In the end, success may look very different, and it may be far better than we ever imagined!

Rigid, narrow, or small outcomes usually bring disappointment. When our dreams are too small, we lose enthusiasm and focus. Instead of the big dream riveting our hearts and energizing our actions, we drift back into the dismal swamp of mediocrity and apathy.

Most of us get stuck on our old, distorted maps, and we aren't open to new possibilities. But two variables push us out of our comfort zones: people and change. Family members, co-workers, and neighbors say and do things that threaten our rigid, narrow way of thinking. We have the choice at that point to react defensively or respond with new thinking, new possibilities, and new hope. Every change in our lives offers the same point of choice. We can react rigidly, or we can respond boldly.

I have an opportunity to respond boldly every weekend at Discover Leadership Training! For example, not long ago, some graduates of our training volunteered to help in our preparation for a weekend. I asked them to put nametags in holders, but one volunteer put the nametags in the holders upside down. When we arrived at the training and gave out the nametags, some people noticed the mistake and turned their own nametags right-side up, but they didn't tell anybody else whose nametags were upside down. Conventional, rigid, narrow thinking would have been to blame the volunteer who made the mistake and tell everybody to check their nametags, but I saw this as a unique opportunity to teach an important lesson—to the volunteer and to everyone else.

Clear outcomes will sharpen your priorities, clarify your choices at each point, and provide tremendous energy on the path to success.

I didn't say anything about the nametags for a while, then I raised the issue and made the observation that few if any in the group told anyone else to fix their upside down nametags. Then I asked, "What are other areas in your life in which you see people in need and fail to speak truth to them?" We had a wonderful, rich discussion, and from that day on, we have been putting people's nametags upside down on purpose! What began as a mistake became a valuable teaching tool. If I had treated it only as a mistake by our volunteers, hundreds of people would have missed the opportunity to learn.

Set your sights high, and don't attempt to choreograph each individual step to the outcomes you have defined. Be open and flexible, with high hopes and an optimistic spirit. The first and most important step is to focus on the outcomes you truly want, your hopes and dreams. Clear outcomes will sharpen your priorities, clarify your choices at each point, and provide tremendous energy on the path to success.

At the end of each chapter, I have included some questions to help you apply the principles I'm imparting to you. Take the time to think, and then write your responses. The discipline of reflecting and writing will force you to wrestle with the principles so that you can apply them specifically and powerfully to your life. There's not much room in this book for you to write your answers. Get a notebook so you'll have plenty of space. You'll be glad you did!

Think About This:

1. WAYFO? means, "What are you focused on?" What are some ways you can tell what someone is really focused on? How will this question help when you have to make an important decision?

2. Reflect on your thinking process for the last big decision you made. How would you describe your "conversation with yourself"? Was it mostly optimistic and hopeful, or was it fearful and negative? Did you spend your mental energies

searching for solutions, or were you oppressed by the "what ifs"? What choices and actions resulted from your thinking? (Did you set clear outcomes and take bold steps to accomplish them, or did you wait for somebody to come to your rescue?)

3. What kind of conversations do you have with yourself about your career? Does that conversation need to change? If so, how?

4. This chapter said that we should pursue our dreams even if other people don't support us or approve. Do you agree or disagree with this statement: "Others' affirmation and assistance are nice, but they're not necessary." Explain your answer.

5. According to this chapter, how can failure be our friend?

6. What are some reasons it's helpful to be open and flexible in defining our dreams and the specific outcomes we want to achieve?

7. How has the conversation you have had with yourself allowed you to hold back? How will you change that conversation? How will it benefit you?

Live Life on Purpose

Better "Ashes than Dust"

One of the most important lessons I've ever learned is this: Never settle for mediocrity. A life of meaning and purpose necessarily involves an element of risk. In fact, if you're not living on the edge, you're taking up too much room!

Novelist Jack London eloquently wrote:

"I would rather be ashes than dust!
I would rather my sparks'
should burn out in a blaze
than it should be stifled by dry-rot.
I would rather be a superb meteor,
every atom of me in magnificent glow,
than asleep and permanent as a planet.
The proper function of a man is to live,
not to exist.

I shall not waste my days *trying* to prolong them. I shall use my time."

Have you ever watched a heart monitor? When it's hooked up to a patient, the heart waves go up and down. That's a good sign, because it means the patient is alive. When you see a flat line on the read-out, that's not so good!

Unfortunately, most people go through life with a flat line on their life's heart monitor. Yes, they're technically alive and breathing, with a heartbeat and a pulse, but a big part of them is dead. They're just showing up and going through the motions instead of experiencing the incredible adventure of living a life of purpose. They accept the little they already have instead of taking responsibility for what they really want. They live their lives waiting to die—they hold back.

We can either be fully alive, or we can be zombies, the walking dead. The choice is ours. We can participate in the game of life, or we can sit on sidelines and let someone else control our experiences. Why would we settle for anything less than living on purpose? We need to take a good, long, hard look at our lives. If we aren't satisfied with what we see, we don't have to just shrug our shoulders and mumble, "What's the use?" **We can grab life by the throat and not let go until we've made a difference!** The path of radical change is an opportunity for incredible growth. Yes, this kind of change will make us uncomfortable, but the area outside our comfort zone is where learning happens.

God gave me a sense of purpose. I listened, and I responded. As I mentioned in the last chapter, that purpose is to have a powerful impact on every person in the world, but the first person who has been powerfully impacted is me. This clear, compelling sense of purpose keeps me

I can measure every activity by whether it takes me a step toward my life's purpose or a step away from it.

focused and clarifies my choices. It shows me what's important and what isn't. I can measure every activity by whether it takes me a step toward my life's purpose or a step away from it. To be honest, I sometimes make dumb choices, but I can't say, "I didn't know what I was doing." I knew perfectly well, and I chose to accept the consequences. No excuses; no denials.

Every morning, I write in my journal to confirm my purpose and build on the opportunities of the day. Each day is my "revenue," and I can invest it any way I choose. The discipline of writing galvanizes my thinking and rivets my mind on the things that are most important. That exercise is like gold to me. I wouldn't give it up for the world. It shapes my attitude and my expectations so that I'm ready for anything and everything.

My attitude determines my outcomes. If I'm pessimistic, even opportunities appear to be obstacles, but if I'm full of hope and optimism, there are no real obstacles because every event and every interaction is an opportunity to learn and grow so that I get a step closer to my ultimate purpose in life. In fact, my perspective is that the Universe is conspiring for my ultimate success!

My Guarantee

Life is so much more than just marking time. I don't know how people stand not being in a growth mode, not focused on how to live life better. I make you a guarantee. If you aren't living your life on purpose, you'll be very unhappy. Write it down. It's a fact. A commitment to grow means making choices and taking risks, but avoiding risks at all costs robs us of passion, limits opportunities, and makes relationships shallow. We live our lives holding back. Who wants to live that way?

It's a big leap to change like this, to have a completely different outlook on every aspect of your life, but when you change your mind, you change your world.

Having a compelling sense of purpose doesn't mean that everything will go well all the time. There are always challenges and tough choices. But a clear purpose creates tremendous, positive energy, and the positive drives out the negative. The strongest energy always prevails.

Most people go through life all hung up on getting from destination to destination, focused on getting this convenience and that pleasure. What happened to the thrill of the journey? Today, people are event-driven, waiting for the next big thing. They focus on when they are out of high school, when they graduate from college, when they get married, when they have kids, when they get the "right" job, when they retire... and then they're dead. What happened? They missed out on life! Real life was happening in between all these events, but they never bothered to notice.

We carry inside us all the things we need to be happy, but too many people never know those things are even there.

Some of us believe that once we've made it through

a particular milestone event, it's over. **I have news for you. It's never over.** Even when you're dead, the choices you made and how you influenced others will live on long after your funeral. You have affected others through your lessons and example, and they will pass it on to others, for better or for worse.

Instead of thinking, "If I can make it to this point in my life, and then I can relax," consider all the choices and opportunities you have before that point. When you're waiting for the next big thing, you're playing the game not to lose instead of playing to win. And playing the game not to lose is like standing on the sidelines not playing at all. That attitude is narrow and negative, waiting for things to happen instead of taking action, focused on everything that can go wrong, and being the flag.

Enjoying the journey means you are an outcome-focused person. You know where you are going, and you are committed to enjoy every step of the process to get there.

"When You Get to a Fork in the Road . . ."

New York Yankees Hall of Fame player Yogi Berra is reported to have said, "When you get to a fork in the road, take it."

When you reach your "fork," or choice points, and

you have clearly defined outcomes, you'll know which direction to go. If your dreams are cloudy and your outcomes are unclear, you'll probably end up taking the easiest way because you won't have a clear sense of which is the right choice.

Your choices create and define you. Your choices say, "This is who I am, and this is what I'm committed to accomplish, regardless of outside factors."

Your choices create and define you. Your choices say, "This is who I am, and this is what I'm committed to accomplish, regardless of outside factors." Or your choices say, "I don't have a clue. I'm just waiting for a good strong wind to blow me in one direction or another."

Living life on purpose offers great benefits. **The #1 payoff of having a clear, strong sense of purpose is that it feels good!** When you know what you want to accomplish, you're far more likely to produce results that you want. When you accomplish each outcome along the way, you feel fulfilled. When you push upstream, go against the tide, and experience success, it feels great!

Let that feeling be your anchor. When you experience the exhilaration of success, build on it, and let it drive you even further so you won't go back to old ways of doing things. Too often people start to change, but then go back to a default mode. Do not let that happen to you. Learn from both failure and success. Both can be stepping-stones to accomplishing your dreams!

Words and Actions

When people go back to default mode they become SAY–DO–BE people. They emphasize words instead of actions, and their focus is their need for you to understand them. They expect you to be just as negative, helpless, and hopeless as they are, and they assume your thoughts are just as self-defeating as theirs. They say things to you over and over again, and when you still don't get it, they repeat the same words—only louder and angrier.

Words are inherently ambiguous. We attach arbitrary meanings to them, and they can be easily misunderstood. To be clear in your communications, BE instead of SAY. When you are "being" and "doing" specific things, your words aren't open to interpretation (or as we so often think, misinterpretation!).

In communication, the actual words play a surprisingly small part in relating a message. Only 7% of our communication are the actual words themselves; the rest is non-verbal, consisting of our tone of voice and gestures. Words can be empty vessels. For example, if you heard a husband say to his wife, "I love you," with tenderness in his voice as he took her hand, you would think that message was authentic. But if you heard him say exactly the same words in a loud, angry tone with his fist shaking in her face, you'd conclude that his actions spoke far louder than his words! If you want to know the measure of a person, look to his or her actions. As it is written in Matthew 7:16, "By their fruits, you shall know them."

You bear fruit by "who you be" far more than by what you say. You live on purpose primarily by your actions. Hopefully, your words will back up your actions. If not, then people have every right to wonder about your motives, integrity, and intentions.

It's Your Choice

You have a choice to live your life on purpose. Maybe you thought you were giving it your all before, but after taking a personal inventory, you may not feel that way. Let me suggest a few questions to prod your thinking:

- Are you the kind of person you would like to work for? If not, why not?

- Is your belief in and your love for your work obvious? If not, why not?
- Is your belief in and your love for your family and friends obvious? If not, why not?
- What kind of an image do you project?
- How do you feel about that image?
- Are you a positive role model? How can you tell?
- When was the last time you learned something new?
- When was the last time you did/explored something different?

Come alive! Open your mind and learn new concepts and skills. Of course, the first step is admitting that you don't know everything. For some people, that's a huge step! When you are humble enough to say, "I need to learn some things," a new world opens up, and your life is enriched, you begin to observe how you are holding back.

Commit to a lifetime of learning and growth. Have you ever looked at a loaf of bread that sat in the breadbox too long? It turns moldy, and so can you!

You are alive, filled with potential and purpose. Have you found yours? Is there a sense of vitality and eagerness in each day? Do you look at problems as opportunities to grow stronger and wiser? If you were to die today, what would people say about you as they stood over your grave?

Those aren't irrelevant questions for you and me today. The answers determine if we are truly alive, or if we are zombies, the walking dead. A strong sense of purpose can come from many different sources. Many of us have internalized the wonderful example of our parents, and we've made their purposes our own. On the other hand, some of us grew up with parents who were poor examples, and we are determined to be different,

You are alive, filled with potential and purpose. Have you found yours? Is there a sense of vitality and eagerness in each day? Do you look at problems as opportunities to grow stronger and wiser?

better, more productive people. Some of us have been captured by great causes to change the world, and some want to make a profound difference in the lives of a few.

Many people have very limited purposes: to get rich, to live a comfortable life, to acquire power over others, or to be popular. Those purposes are common, but they are ultimately empty. Many years ago, John D. Rockefeller was the richest man in the world. He was asked by a newspaper reporter, "Mr. Rockefeller, what will it take for you to be happy." The wealthiest man in the world told her, "Just a little bit more. Just a little bit more."

Riches, power, prestige, and popularity feel good for a while, but ultimately, they leave us empty and lonely. I encourage you to find a sense of purpose that is bigger—far bigger—than yourself. If you don't have that kind of purpose today, keep pursuing your heart until you have one. Nothing in the world is more important! When you have one, it will transform every fiber of your being. You'll make any sacrifice, pay any price, and go anywhere to accomplish the purpose that's burned into your heart. You will hold nothing back from reaching that outcome.

Think About This:

1. Read Jack London's poem again. Does his passion reflect your heart? Why or why not?
2. Why is it important to enjoy each step of the journey, not just the destination?
3. Describe a time when you fulfilled an important outcome in your life. How did you feel during the process? How did you feel at the end?
4. I've heard someone say, "You can tell what a person's purpose is by looking at his checkbook

and his schedule." Do you agree or disagree with that statement? Explain your answer.

5. Why is it crucial that our purpose is bigger than our own pleasure, success, and comfort?

6. Who are a few people (even just one!) who are the best examples of those who model a life of passionate, compelling purpose?

7. Take some time to think and reflect on your own purpose. Write it here.

8. Does your statement of purpose have "the ring of truth" to it? Does it feel right, good, and strong, or do you need to think about it more? If you're still working on it, how will you know when it's really your own?

C H A P T E R 3

Create the Will, the Way Will Come

Vision and Determination

I came across a Chinese proverb that eloquently stated: "When your cart reaches the foot of the mountain, a path will appear." In the same way, your path will appear when you create the will and muster the courage to move forward to accomplish the outcomes you want. Vision and determination are the essence of a person's will. People may have a clear vision, but if they don't have the determination to pursue it through thick and thin, they'll quit when they encounter obstacles, which are inevitable in every person's life.

Years ago, I applied to become a Houston Police Helicopter Pilot, but the department recruiter told me that I had to join the Police Department before they would consider me for that position. They also informed me that I didn't stand a snowball's chance in Hell of ever being assigned to that division. There were several reasons. First, tradition required applicants to have at least 10 years on the police department, secondly and most important you had to know somebody who could pull some strings. Despite the history lesson and the discouragement from the recruiters, I joined the Houston Police Department.

I had a vision of what I wanted to do, and I was determined to reach the outcome I wanted. Nothing was going to stop me, not empty tradition or any messages of doom. I completed my first year, and after some serious struggles with the department, I remained focused on my outcome and held nothing back. As a result, I became a proud member of the Houston Police Department Helicopter Division. I served there for 12 years.

Create a New Map

When your vision is strong and clear, don't attempt to plan every step of the way to get there. Planning is essential. However, you shouldn't be too narrow or rigid. Be open to new ideas, new skills, and new perspectives. Remember that you began the journey with an old, faulty map. Yes, you have already made some changes to your mental map of assumptions and beliefs so you could chart your new vision in the first place. But the job of redrawing your map isn't finished—by a long shot! Your old map still has faulty perceptions about people, yourself, and the way life works. As you take steps toward the outcome you envision, you'll challenge those faulty perceptions. At each point, you'll have the chance (and the choice) to confront and correct them.

I've talked to a lot of successful men and women who laughed and shook their heads as they told me about their progress toward fulfilling their vision. One of them told me, "You wouldn't believe all I've learned since I started 15 years ago. I thought I had everything nailed down and airtight back then, but I had a lot to learn. Over the years, I faced a hundred roadblocks, and every one of them has taught me a valuable lesson. Today, I'm much wiser than I was when I started." That's a fantastic description of someone who has redrawn his map!

If you insist on creating something new by using only your old map, you'll be terribly frustrated, and you'll fail. Obstacles and disappointments aren't tragedies unless they stop us. They are wonderful opportunities to step back, analyze what we believe, learn new truths, and redraw our perceptions and expectations.

Naturally, you will benefit from your education, skills, wisdom, and experience. Those are important tools in the toolbox and develop the courage to build on these things instead of being satisfied with them. **Press forward, learn, grow, and develop fresh insights and skills.**

When we plan well and remain open to new possibilities, it's amazing how many helpful people, encouraging events, and positive changes appear on our radar screens. The simple act of focusing on our desired outcomes with openness and optimism is like a magnet for good things to come our way.

> **The simple act of focusing on our desired outcomes with openness and optimism is like a magnet for good things to come our way.**

If we have tunnel vision, we will insist on things going exactly a certain way to accomplish exactly the outcomes we have envisioned. That narrow focus severely limits our ability to grasp and take advantage of fresh, new, exciting possibilities. If we step back, however, and open our hearts and minds, we'll see all kinds of options. Then amazing things happen, and we'll take giant strides toward fulfilling our vision.

To take advantage of new possibilities, we can't close doors or focus on potential obstacles. There are plenty of negative, pessimistic, fearful people who want to keep us exactly in our—and their—comfort zones. But we initially set out on this journey because we chose to! Critics may shout, "You can't," or "This won't work," but they can't stop you. Don't give them permission and power to hold you back.

Words have a tremendous impact on us—for good or bad. The labels we assign to people and situations determine how we respond to them. We are conditioned to believe that certain words are negative, no matter how we *try* to explain them. For example, the word "criticism" is universally seen as painful. Even when we add the adjective "constructive," most people still believe it will hurt more than it will help. Similarly, if we think of somebody as a "jerk," we'll have great difficulty valuing anything that person says or does. Or if we label one of our efforts as a "failure," we will be tempted to deny it, blame somebody else, or make excuses. For this reason, I seldom use the word "failure." Instead, I see every situation as a wonderful opportunity to help people take a step of growth. Some of these opportunities are fun, pleasant, and obvious, but the most teachable moments in our lives are cleverly disguised as problems. Our attitude (and the label we assign to these moments) determines if these are stepping stones or roadblocks.

When I began Discover Leadership Training, I was convinced that I didn't have skills in marketing and sales, so I hired a group of salespeople. As the weeks and months went on, they simply weren't getting the job done. I was convinced that the principles I wanted to teach were revolutionary, but they wouldn't do anybody any good if I couldn't get people to the training. I had a choice. I could panic and blame my staff, or I could use this critical moment to analyze our organization and make necessary changes. I had clearly defined the outcome I wanted our organization to achieve, but we weren't getting there. Doing the same thing over and over again wasn't going to get us there, either. To get different results, we had to make significant changes.

As I reflected on the reality of our situation, I realized that Discover Leadership Training is primarily a sales organization that conducts outstanding training events, not a training organization that has to sell it's services. That may not sound like much of change to you, but it was a monumental shift in my own map and the perspective of each person on our team. We didn't see the situation as a failure and panic. Instead, we saw it as a wonderful opportunity to reinvent ourselves. And Discover has prospered since that day.

No Limits

Some of us become far too preoccupied with the exact steps we need to take to reach our outcomes. If we focus too much on those individual steps, we'll become anxious and lose our enthusiasm. Fear and worry will take over. Then, instead of "I can!" we may start thinking, "I can't." And we won't!

Create the right conversations in your mind—a positive conversation, holding nothing back, no limits and no barriers. Self-doubt can creep in and convince you that you are doomed to fail, or that you lack the tools or the education

If you're committed to giving 100% of what you have to give, look forward to an exciting, positive journey.

necessary to reach your desired outcomes. When you allow your fears to rule your thoughts and actions, they send you in another direction—always the wrong one.

Your focus has to be that it will happen, not how it will happen. You may have a general idea about the direction you need to go. However, I assure you, there will be surprises along the way. **If you're committed to giving 100% of what you have to give, look forward to**

an exciting, positive journey.

The way will appear when we have the will to take bold steps. The big question is, "Do you trust yourself that much?"

Imagine you are high up in a mountain. You have the will to make it from this side of the mountain to the other side, but a huge ravine blocks your path. You're with a partner you trust, but you're blindfolded. You can't see a thing. Your partner says, "The ravine is really deep. No one could fall into it and come out alive. We're coming to a bridge. Trust me. It's time to take that first step onto the bridge."

How do you step into something you can't see? Trust doesn't say, "I hear what you're saying, partner, but I have to be sure. I'm going to lay down here and try to feel the whole bridge before I take a step." That's not trust. Trust is a solid first step, willing to put your life on the line.

A determined will gives you courage to trust your partner and take steps to make it to the other side. You may never see the way, but as long as you remain focused on the outcome, you'll move toward it. The way will come because every step you take will create a new choice point that brings you closer. As long as you have the determination to keep taking steps, those choice points will keep coming.

Many of us face ravines in our lives, and we exclaim, "But, I don't know what will happen next!" Anxiety floods our hearts. We want to be in control, and in fact, we demand to be in control! Control, we are sure, is the cure for our fears. The truth, though, is that any control you *think* you possess is an illusion. Your worry won't control the future. The truth is that none of us knows what will happen next.

Our faulty maps tell us that we have to be in control so we can feel safe and secure. And we demand more control as we feel more insecure. In those situations, some of us become obsessed with minutia of plans and checklists so we can feel like we're in total control of our lives. That kind of reaction to difficult situations forces us to become narrow, ingrown, and even more fearful.

When we feel out of control, instead of becoming fearful and narrow, we need to respond in the opposite way. We need to open our minds to new possibilities and use our emotional energy to take courageous steps. As I have mentioned, this is a fantastic opportunity to recognize parts of our maps that are faulty and destructive. At these pivotal moments, we can change what we believe about ourselves and about life.

Those who use their emotional energy to take courageous steps have the attitude: "I don't care what comes next because I'm determined to conquer it. I'll handle anything that comes my way!"

Isn't that a better way to live?

Running To and From

When you focus on the will to succeed, you'll move in the right direction. At the same time, you need to discard anything that doesn't fit with your guiding principles. Remove stumbling blocks, and replace them with strength and hope. No one else can do that for you.

When you are running to, you are creating the will to succeed. The combination of determination and enthusiasm is a powerfully positive force in shaping the direction of your life!

You are either *running to* what you want, or you are *running away* from what you don't want. Running toward an outcome is exciting, but running away from potential destruction saps your energy and consumes your mind with negative, fearful thoughts.

The choice is yours, and that choice makes a huge impact on how you feel and behave. **When you are running to, you are creating the will to succeed.** The combination of determination and enthusiasm is a powerfully positive force in shaping the direction of your life!

Running to moves you in the right direction—always forward.

When you're running from, you're looking over your shoulder, running scared, bumping into things, tripping and falling. Most people live like this, running from something they don't want or don't like. When you're running from something, you're living in *survival mode*. You're in *thriving mode* when you're running to something. You're achieving something that you haven't done before, and that's pretty darn exciting!

Most people on diets are running from. Their mantra is, "I have to stop eating so much." That's the wrong conversation, because what gets your attention gets you. "I have to stop eating so much" conjures up images of . . . eating! But when you're dieting, food is the last thing you want on your mind. Running away from food, then, is a self-defeating strategy. The better strategy is to run to healthy choices. This strategy says, "I'm focused on eating healthy dinners for the next 30 days. I'm running to something positive. I created the will to get healthier, and the way will come."

All dieters face tough choices. They have to ask, "What actions should I take? I'll plan my meals, but my old behavioral patterns are part of my subconscious, and they are telling me to grab a burger in a sack on my way home because I'm hungry!"

There's a choice point here. When you change a behavior, you have to act consciously and deliberately at every step you take. Your level of awareness of your feelings and choices in the present moment must be clear before you will do something different. Old patterns of behavior will only take you to a place you don't want to go.

So focus on what you want. Find a picture of yourself at the weight you want to be, and imagine how good you will look in that new outfit you saw in the magazine! Even if you don't know from first-hand experience, picture it. Visualize choices that will get you closer to your desired outcomes. Then you're running to those outcomes, and you're no longer running from food.

One good habit multiplies itself. When you're running to healthy eating, you'll find yourself also running to other aspects of healthy living, such as getting better sleep. You'll run to better work habits, more time with friends, a new hobby, and other positive outcomes in every area of your life. Sounds pretty good, doesn't it? The outcome is to overcome negative behaviors and create new behaviors that will get you to your outcomes. Then you'll make the choices that are consistent with those outcomes, always focusing on the positives, not just on avoiding the problem.

When you shift your thinking to running to, everyone in your environment begins to shift with you. You'll create an environment of positive changes. You'll notice a shift in your own and others' language, outlook, and attitude. When you think and act more positively, you'll have a powerful impact on those around you. You'll be amazed at the people who tell you they want to be a part of whatever you're doing!

A New Look at Habits

Sometimes I tell people, "A habit is a habit when it isn't a habit." Yes, I'm well aware that this statement sounds like gibberish, but I have an important point to make. We think of habits as behaviors that are ironclad, ingrained, and unchangeable, that's not the case at all. Each repeatable behavior, commonly known as a habit, is a collection of individual choices. Many of us have *tried* to break bad habits, but we give up because we're convinced that they are far too difficult to break. If we see each component part, however, we'll see that we have clear, distinct choices all along the way. That insight makes it far easier to make decisions and change those behaviors.

Let me give you an illustration. A person who

smokes has to drive to the store to buy a package of cigarettes. He has to have money set aside for the purchase, and he has to physically pick up the package and take it to the counter to buy it. He has to take the cigarette out of the package. He has to find a match. He has to light the match. Finally, he has to light up, inhale, and take that smoke into his body. That's a lot of choice points where different decisions could have been made. He could stop, evaluate, and make a determination whether he is accomplishing his outcomes, based on his life's purpose. Those choices aren't rigid, ingrained habits. They are a collection of individual moments of decision.

A rule of thumb is that if we can personally observe our habit, then it's not a habit. It's a choice point. The vast majority of "bad habits" are collections of bad choices, but some behaviors fall into a different category. Some people believe cigarette smoking is only a bad habit. I don't believe that. I believe it's usually an addiction, and an addiction is far more difficult to change than a habit.

Repetitive behaviors become a part of our subconscious thinking. Sooner or later, we do things simply because we've done them before. That's what habits are all about. To change those repetitive behaviors, we have to identify the individual, specific choices we make. Then we can make different decisions and break the habit. Change begins with surfacing our thoughts so we can analyze them, confront them, and make better choices.

Each small change will build new behaviors when you focus on your desired outcome. Sometimes, people need an incentive to help them make a better choice. I knew a smoker who said she wanted to stop, and she was willing to make the conscious effort. I told her I'd help her, so I made a deal with her. Every time she smoked, she had to pay me $100. Shortly after we made that arrangement, she lit up a cigarette. I smiled and held out my hand. At first, she looked shocked. She hadn't even thought about her choice before she lit up. She shook her head and handed me the $100 (which I gave to charity). This woman never smoked again. That choice got a little too expensive for her!

To get rid of bad habits, make a commitment to pursue a clear, specific outcome. Here are some recommendations:

- Get an accountability partner who is someone you really trust and with whom you are willing to be open and honest. Communicate your desired outcome with this person, and ask her to hold your feet to the fire.

- Identify the habit you want to eliminate. If you missed dinner with your family every night for two weeks and you're feeling bad about that behavior, tell your accountability partner about it.

- Be specific about creating new behaviors by having clear outcomes. What are you going to do about it? In the example about missing too many dinners with your family, you can't just say, "I'm going to work fewer hours." That won't cut it. A clearer outcome might be: "I'm going to limit my work week to 50 hours, and I'll be home by 5:30 at least three days a week."

- Then, be more specific about how you will use your time with your family. For example, "I'm going to use that time to give my children three hours of homework support, two hours of fun, and I'm going to take my spouse on a date every Wednesday night." Now, that's something you can do!

- Hold yourself accountable. That first week you work 55 hours, instead of your usual 70. That's a big improvement, so give yourself a hand! You're still working toward the outcome you want, but you're not yet there. Hold yourself accountable by writing down a specific agreement. Give a copy to your accountability partner.

- Have real consequences. If I had told my friend she would have to pay me $1,000 every time she smoked, she would have laughed at the absurdity of that consequence. She couldn't afford it (and I wouldn't have taken the money anyway). $100 was painful but reasonable. The consequences you set must be realistic.

When you fail, you won't get off the hook with a simple, "I'm sorry," or "I'll *try* harder next week." That won't cut it. I've heard politicians say, "I'm sorry, I take full responsibility for that blunder," but they suffer no consequences for their failure, and they take no steps toward restoring broken relationships or making amends with those they've wronged. They haven't taken responsibility at all, and my guess is that the only thing they're sorry about is that they got caught.

Consequences can be positive or negative. Rewards for progress are just as important as costs for failures. Any positive progress deserves a standing ovation. **When you take steps forward, get excited about it! Celebrate!**

Measure your progress solely on your own standard

of performance. Don't judge your success by others' yardsticks because you don't know what obstacles they're overcoming or how much help they're receiving. When you compare yourself to someone else, you run the risk of being too easy or too harsh with yourself.

Set your standard as the best you have ever done, and commit yourself to reaching that outcome. Don't compare yourself with others, and don't let others' success or failure get you off track.

Ask your accountability partner to help you establish consequences based on standards that fit you and your situation. For example, it may take one person a month to lose five pounds, but it may take someone else only a week. Some people decide they will never smoke again, and they can go cold turkey from the first day. For others, it's a yearlong battle with many ups and downs. The only thing that matters is your progress. When you are holding yourself 100% accountable for your progress, you're doing great!

If you look outside yourself to determine how well you're doing, you're setting yourself up for failure. At that point, some people get discouraged and quit. The only barometer you need is your own standard. Set your standard as *the best you have ever done*, and commit yourself to reaching that outcome. Don't compare yourself with others, and don't let others' success or failure get you off track.

When we harshly condemn ourselves for not measuring up to someone's arbitrary standard, our children are watching our example. By watching us, they learn tenacity to keep pursuing a good outcome even when the going gets tough, or they learn to complain, blame others, and quit. Comparing ourselves to others teaches them the wrong lesson. It's even worse when we compare our kids to other children. I've heard parents bark at their children, "Why aren't you making A's like little Johnny across the street? You're not applying yourself like he is! You'd better shape up!"

There are many reasons why children don't get the same grades other kids receive. Every child, even those in the same family from the same gene pool, experience different styles of learning, different teachers, and different abilities. They aren't encouraged or helped by comparing them with other children. They are positively challenged when we hold them accountable to their own personal best.

Negative comparisons are destructive, but even positive comparisons can limit our drive and success.

Some of us look around at others and conclude, "Hey, I'm doing pretty well. Compared to my neighbors, I have a better job, a better car, a bigger house, and a nicer boat. There's no need to sweat about doing any better." With that attitude, we use positive comparisons as an excuse for "good-nuf."

Resist the temptation to compare yourself—favorably or harshly—to others, and don't make the mistake of comparing your family members to others, either. One of the painful results of comparison is that it reaps what it sows, and we are compared (usually harshly) with others' behavior, appearance, and character.

Judge yourself only by your own standards of excellence. Your focus should be riveted on being better today than you were yesterday. When you get up every day, truly committed to giving your personal best, making choices in line with the outcomes you want to achieve, and giving 100% of yourself, old "habits" will die. They may die hard, but they'll die. Don't let bad "habits" get the best of you. Dissolve them into their component parts, see the choices clearly, and make better decisions. That simple solution can change your life!

Think About This:

1. Explain why it's more important to have a determined will than to have the path to success clearly defined.

2. In what ways can disappointments and obstacles be used to redraw our mental maps?

3. Do you agree or disagree with this statement?
   The simple act of focusing on our desired outcomes with openness and optimism is like a magnet for good things to come our way.
   Explain your answer.

4. What are some of the benefits of keeping an open heart and mind as you strive toward reaching the outcomes you want to achieve?

5. What is the connection between our fear and an inordinate need to control things, people, and events? In what ways does your fear drive your need to control?

6. Describe a time in your life when you have had this attitude: "I don't care what comes next because I'm determined to conquer it. I'll handle anything that comes my way!"

7. Describe the importance of running to a positive outcome instead of running away from a negative one.

8. Do you have a bad habit that you've had trouble breaking? If so, what is it? Based on the principles in this chapter, describe your plan of action to break the habit into its component parts, identify your choices, make good decisions, hold yourself accountable, and implement consequences for your performance.

C H A P T E R 4

Breaking the Bonds of Fear

False Evidence Appearing Real

F... E...A...R. False Evidence Appearing Real. Of course, there are real threats to us that prompt rational, reasoned responses of fear (such as a robber in the house or a tractor-trailer hurtling toward us on the freeway), but in most cases, our fear is the product of faulty assumptions in our thinking. That's all it is. If we can identify those faulty assumptions and the false evidence, most of our fear will melt away!

Too often, people are ruled by fear, and since September 11, 2001, we seem to be experiencing an even heavier dose of anxiety. We all want to be "secure," but complete and absolute security is an illusion. Consider the words of Helen Keller, who said, "Security is mostly a superstition. It does not exist in nature. Nor do children of men as a whole experience it. Avoiding danger is no safer in the long run than outright exposure."

Many people let fear stop them from making bold decisions and taking action that benefit them and those they love. Their fear is a huge barrier to fulfilling, successful lives. They allow their fears to drain them emotionally and keep them locked in situations where they aren't happy. Others around them can easily see that these unhappy people are stuck in the mud of doubt and dread. Why don't they see it? Why don't you and I see it in <u>ourselves</u>?

Look at your whole life, personally and professionally. Is everything going the way you want it to go? Or are you just accepting the little you *have* instead of accepting responsibility to go after what you *want?* Why are you holding back?

Inordinate fear is an illusion that only exists in the conversation you are having with yourself. The "tapes" of doubt we've heard over and over again are like a straightjacket. We listen to them over and over again, and we feel trapped, powerless to change. Many of these tapes have our parents' voices.

As a child, your mother may have reprimanded you for going outside without your jacket when it was cold. Then, when you got sick, mother reminded you that you went outside without your jacket. What's her evidence? Cold air made you sick. Now, as an adult, you make your children bundle up when it is 60 degrees and sunny. After all, who wants their children to get sick? Sure, there are reports that prove bacteria cause colds and flu, not weather, however, you were taught that your mother knew best. After all, she had the evidence: You got sick a couple of times.

But this is false evidence. As soon as you muster the courage to challenge the "truths" you've been taught and step outside your comfort zone, you'll find out that some of those "truths" are, in fact, false. Because these perceptions of life, God, and people have been ingrained in us during our formative years, most of us cling our whole lives to false evidence about what and whom we should fear.

The antidote to fear is committing to outcomes you want and moving toward them.

It's not magic. On your way to these outcomes, you'll face many clear choice points along the way. When you get to each choice point, you'll make a decision to follow truth or falsehood. Following truth can be difficult. If we have believed for 30, 40, or 50 years that life works a certain way, it takes immense courage to move down a different path.

The key is to clearly define the outcomes you want to achieve, focus on the benefits of those outcomes, and take steps—big or small—toward them. Tough choices aren't always comfortable, but if you're convinced they are in alignment with your outcomes, you're much more likely to make the right decisions.

If you don't define your outcomes (and the benefits you'll enjoy from those outcomes), you may complain about your situation and you'll stay right where you are. Instead of moving forward to take advantage of new opportunities, you'll continue to suffer from feelings of helplessness, apathy, and failure.

Tough choices aren't always comfortable, but if you're convinced they are in alignment with your outcomes, you're much more likely to make the right decisions.

Suffering is not cool! Do you really want to say to yourself, "This situation is not what I want. This is not who I want to be." and continue holding back doing the same, unproductive things? To break out of the old paradigm of feeling like a victim in your painful circumstances, you have to get tough. You have to have a bulldog mentality that you're going to change— no holding back no matter what!

When you choose *tough* over *suffering*, you're

willing to confront your old thinking, your old habits, and your old choices. Most people, though, let their fear dominate their lives. Things drag on and on until they get angry or depressed, then they react and make another bad decision. It would have been far better to recognize the need to change, think it through, and then make reasoned decisions to move strongly and directly toward the new outcomes they have defined.

Rollo May was acquainted with fear. He experienced a painful childhood, and he suffered from tuberculosis. Through his reflections about his own emotional and physical pain, he became a champion of personal bravery. He wrote, "The hallmark of courage in our age of conformity is the capacity to stand on one's convictions—not obstinately or defiantly (these are gestures of defensiveness, not courage) nor as a gesture of retaliation, but simply because these are what one believes."

Excuses

Of course, we have plenty of excuses to stay stuck in fear. Some of us are afraid of rejection. We think, "Oh, I don't want to get anyone mad at me!" And some people believe their new choices will hurt others. They think, "I don't want people to feel bad, so I won't do anything to upset them." Still others are simply afraid that they'll fail in their new pursuits. They wonder, "What if I *try* this new way, and I mess it up? I can't handle that!"

Those are the excuses of doubt and fear. We aren't in control of anyone else's emotions or actions—only our own. We don't make someone else feel bad. That's their choice, not ours. Of course, when we change, those close to us may feel uncomfortable. That's simply the nature of change. In most cases, people are far more frustrated with us when we are irresponsible or overly responsible than when we clearly define our responsibilities and stick with them. Speaking the truth about others and ourselves (with tact, of course) is an important part of our responsibility. **Honesty and open communication helps every one involved—them and us—clarify our responsibilities and take steps of change.**

How often have you "tried" to spare someone's feelings? How often does that really work? Avoiding the truth creates its own tension. We know we are hiding something, and people around us sense we aren't being authentic. Still, most of us choose to remain in this uncomfortable state of tension instead of having honest conversations that bring resolution.

To Confront or Not to Confront?

Do you realize how people appreciate it when you give them positive feedback and ways to grow through "confrontation?" Confrontation isn't a bad thing. If it's done with respect, it's a very good thing.

Let me give you a simple example. You see someone with spinach stuck in his teeth. Do you tell him? Most people wouldn't. They don't want to "embarrass" him. But they'll let this poor guy walk around like this all day! I've heard about people walking around dragging toilet paper on their shoes or wearing their shirts inside out all day, but no one would tell them. And people think they're being kind by not telling these folks the truth! The reality is that these people are being selfish and cruel. I sure want somebody to tell me when my zipper's down or I have bird poop on my suit. I consider those people—even if they're strangers—to be true friends.

The same principle applies in your personal relationships. When you don't confront people with the truth, things get out of balance in your home, at work, and in your life. Negative conversations occur in your mind and with other people. The quicker you confront and speak the truth, the quicker you get agreement, and the faster you move on. By confronting the issue with integrity and honesty, you remove all that tension and misunderstanding.

Most people measure the success or failure of confrontations by the response of the other person. If the person responds well, we feel successful, but if the person rejects us, we believe we've failed. But this is the wrong way to look at it. When I have the courage and compassion to speak the truth to someone, I'm not responsible for the other person's response. I'm only responsible for my honesty, my communication, and my choice to speak up. This is the difference between *managing a promise* and *managing expectations*. Before I learned to build trust as a platform for truth, the process didn't work for other people or for me! I was *trying* to manage my expectations and *make* them respond positively.

> **When I have the courage and compassion to speak the truth to someone, I'm not responsible for the other person's response. I'm only responsible for my honesty, my communication, and my choice to speak up.**

Years ago, I used to get upset if people didn't respond well. If they ignored me, I talked louder and more aggressively, and if they rejected me, I got angry and blasted them back. I saw myself as God's messenger with God's message to help these people. I was ready and able to speak truth into their lives, and if I had to, I was committed to make them respond positively. If they didn't receive it gladly and immediately, I took it as a personal offense! I was *trying* to manage my expectations of others through demands and anger. Instead of building relationships with people, I was destroying them.

I've learned a different way, a far more positive way, to speak the truth to people by managing promises. First, I ask permission to speak to them. If they don't give it, I don't proceed. If they give it (and they almost always do), I speak with calm boldness with the desire to genuinely help them. **My objective is not to make them respond a certain way, <u>instead</u>, I find common ground so we can make promises to each other.** I promise to do some things to help them take steps toward success, and they promise to make changes in their attitudes and actions. We work together to find a solution. This way, our communication isn't a power struggle; it's friendly negotiations. We aren't adversaries; we're partners.

Let me give you an illustration of how I've learned to manage promises instead of managing expectations. A couple of years ago, I worked with someone whose personality is very different from mine. She is analytical, methodical, and slow to make decisions. I (as you might be able to guess) live at a slightly faster pace. I expected some things to get done that weren't happening, so one day, I decided to talk to her about them. I explained what wasn't going well, and I outlined some steps to resolve the problems. She nodded and said she agreed, but her objective in that moment was to get the conversation over as quickly as possible, not to resolve the problems I was talking about! As you can imagine, her performance didn't change at all because she wasn't even listening to me.

After more weeks and months of difficulties, the inevitable happened. She experienced a catastrophe! But like so many others, catastrophe was the catalyst for change in her life. Finally, she was willing and able to listen, and finally, she implemented steps of change.

She wasn't the only one who learned from this give-and-take. I learned that I had to create an atmosphere of trust so people could receive the truth I wanted to communicate. Before, I thought raw, unadulterated truth was enough, and if others didn't respond by accepting my input, I got angry. Working with this dear lady taught me that my tone and mode of communication could make people accept or reject my message. Part of my responsibility—probably the biggest part—is to earn people's trust so they'll listen. As I learned this important lesson, my anger subsided, and our relationship became one of trust instead of a power struggle. We made promises to each other, and we kept them. Finally, we were true partners. ⌣

We need to develop the habit of confronting people with truth earlier rather than later, and then learn from the situation. By speaking the truth sooner, we get the relationship back into balance and move out of suffering. Each of us needs to learn the skill to address the things in our lives that cause pain. Confronting the pain gives us the opportunity to eliminate it, and we learn from the pain so that it doesn't reoccur and re-infect us. Once we do this, we continue to move forward and create new possibilities in our lives and our relationships.

Make no mistake: Confrontation brings anxiety, sweaty palms, and increased heart rate. But the same biological responses happen when you're happy and excited. **When you confront doubt, fear, and misunderstanding, you can then gain an agreement. Then the relief will be amazing!**

Most of us avoid confrontation because we *think* we are going to feel terrible when we do it. We tell ourselves that nothing good can possibly come from speaking the truth to that person, and we find a zillion excuses to avoid the moment of confrontation. Conversations based on fear and doubt don't produce good outcomes. The first step then, is to confront our own negative thinking!

Consider this situation, which sometimes happens when a relationship is over. Your former significant other comes to you and tells you every terrible, awful, horrible thing she thought for years, but never told you when you were together. You ask, "Why now? Why didn't you tell me this before when we could work on it?"

The answer is: "Well, now that we're splitting up, I don't have anything to lose!"

"Sure," you might respond, "but we have nothing to win now, either!"

It's foolish to wait until it's "over"–until it's "comfortable" to say what we have to say. But by then, months, years, and decades of opportunities are lost forever. Fear has crippled our lives and the relationships we hold dear. That's not real life; it's only a bland, empty survival mode. It's living life in 4' x 4' cell. We are imprisoned by our fear of loss, fear of rejection, fear of failure, and even our fear of feeling afraid.

Instead of speaking honestly to offer a meaningful, rich relationship with someone, we hide, play it safe, and miss out on everything rewarding in personal give-

and-take. When we have the courage to speak the truth with others, one of three things can happen. They can accept it, decline it, or ask to negotiate it. That's the full range of possibilities. What's so scary about that?

Instead, most people keep the conflict to themselves, thinking it's better that way. Do you know what happens? The fear, anger, and doubt fester inside them. They suffer silently, losing confidence and hope each day because they replay the negative tapes, and they continue the negative conversation in their minds.

This suffering won't stop until you stop it. To think properly about the situation, ask yourself two questions:

- What have you gained through avoidance?
- Why are you holding back?
- What will you gain through honesty and courage?

I've seen many people suffer terribly in painful relationships. They were willing to put up with abuse, abandonment, and mistreatment, just so they could stay connected to that other person. Their outcome is to avoid feeling alone. They may have dreamed of a day when that other person treated them with respect and love, and they hoped it would happen by magic.

It won't. Resolution and change in relationships only happen when one of the people has the courage to speak the truth to the other and follow through with commitments to truth and integrity. No, that path isn't easy, but it's the only one that offers any hope of real progress. Believing in magic is for fairy tales, not real life.

> **Resolution and change in relationships only happen when one of the people has the courage to speak the truth to the other and follow through with commitments to truth and integrity.**

I've known young women who stayed in abusive relationships only because they wanted to have a boyfriend. But grown ups don't do much better. Many suffer terribly in painful, manipulative relationships. They have bad self-images, seeing themselves as hopeless losers, but they are too afraid to leave a relationship even though it's ruining their lives. They make the choice to continue a life of suffering because they're shackled by their fear. I'm convinced that many of these relationships can take strong steps forward toward honesty, respect, and genuine love if—and only if—someone has the courage to start the process, to confront the sickness of the relationship, and to stand strong as change slowly unfolds.

Confronting others is tough. It calls on a part of you that may have been dormant far too long. But remember, we have those two choices every day, tough ones that lead to hope, or fearful ones that lead to more suffering.

Perhaps you have an employee who isn't doing well and actually is hurting the performance of the rest of the team. You like this person and consider her a friend, but her impact on your business is really starting to show. What do you do?

Should you take the easy path and just say to yourself, "Well, that's just Barbara. Gotta love her." Do you let your team continue to suffer because you are afraid of the tension that would surface if you speak the truth to Barbara? Are you willing to let your bottom line suffer because you keep giving in to your fear? Are you willing to let the morale of the team suffer? Are you willing to let your relationship with Barbara continue to suffer because living in constant tension is preferable than confrontation, resolution, and real growth? All of these things will continue to suffer simply because you choose to be "nice" by avoiding the tension caused by speaking the truth.

Or will you choose to be tough? You can have the courage to bring the problem out in the open and listen to different perspectives that may enlighten you. **Together, you choose to set standards, gain agreements, and move forward.**

Every time I choose to be tough in the work environment, we all benefit. The team communicates better, relationships grow stronger, people figure out if they are working in the right place, and they appreciate my direction in making that happen.

Too many people tell me they don't want to confront—even if they know they're right—because it's scary! They won't even confront their spouses or significant others with whom they have had relationships for years. I really question the trust level there. Serious work needs to be done to change the course of these relationships.

Confronting others with respect and truth means taking a risk, and most people would simply rather not take that risk. When they get to those important choice points, they choose continued suffering.

Outcomes and Change

As I have said many times, defining new, bold positive outcomes is the crucial first step toward change. When we know what we want, and when we are convinced that the benefits of change outweigh the inertia of staying stuck in suffering, we will hold nothing back.

If you want something passionately enough, you'll jump in the water to get to the other side. Just because swimming isn't on your map doesn't mean you can't get to the other side. Jump in the water. If you really want to get to the other side, you'll figure out how to swim!

Many people admit they're afraid about the future, and that fear inevitably leads to anxious thoughts and worry. We see the fruits of anxiety . . . frequent headaches and stomach problems—and more significantly, heart attacks, high blood pressure, and strokes. Those medical problems used to be "men's diseases," but women are gaining ground. In fact, heart disease is the #1 killer of women in this country today.

Negative conversations in our minds can dwell on the "what ifs" and "if onlys." We daydream about all the things that can go wrong, and our anxiety multiplies. None of us knows the future, and even if we did, the distorted thinking from our old maps would create fear instead of hope, passivity instead of courage.

If you knew the future and attempted to line it up your way, you would probably still be disappointed. You would become obsessed with planning every little detail, as if your efforts could control what will happen next. You can't control the future. You can control your response in this present moment.

What are your fears? Do you struggle with the fear of failure? If you don't clearly define the outcomes you want, you have already failed! Do you suffer from the fear of rejection? If you aren't reaching out to people, you're already alone.

Be aware of who you let into your circle. Surround yourself with positive, bold people who challenge your thinking and encourage you to take steps of courage.

A big step toward living without fear is surrounding yourself with positive people. Face it. There are people out there who prefer to see you stay afraid and fail. Be aware of who you let into your circle. Surround yourself with positive, bold people who challenge your thinking and encourage you to take steps of courage.

When I'm on mile 16 of the Houston Marathon, I want people out there shouting, "The finish line is in sight, Mike! You're gonna make it! You're doing great!" I don't invite the folks who would tell me, "Oh, Mike, you're not looking too good! You know, it would be good for you to slow down. In fact, maybe you should just quit."

Who are the people and what are the voices that

surround you? Positive energy and positive people defeat fear. Positive energy and positive people create positive results.

Shift your mindset from fear to confidence. You are powerful. You can overcome anything! Believe in yourself. The people you care about believe in you.

You have nothing to fear. Simply check the conversation you are having with yourself. If that conversation will not produce the results you want— change it.

Think About This:

1. What are some fears people experience? What are some ways these fears affect their lives?

2. Think back on the messages your parents spoke to you and modeled for you. What were the messages of hope and courage that are now "tapes" you listen to in your mind? What are the messages of doubt and fear?

3. Which of these tapes do you hear most often? How do these affect you? What would your life be like if these tapes were replaced by new, positive, bold, hopeful tapes?

4. Describe the ways that living in fear and not confronting painful realities with truth makes us

truly "suffer"?

5. Describe a time when you successfully confronted someone with truth and respect. What kind of mental preparation did you go through?

6. What have you gained through avoiding confrontations?

7. What will you gain through confronting people with honesty and courage?

8. Why is defining desired outcomes an important factor in giving us the direction and motivation we need to speak the truth to someone?

9. Who are the people in your life who challenge and encourage you? Are you spending enough time with them? Explain your answer.

10. As you have read this chapter, have any people come to mind with whom you've been playing games instead of having honest, respectful communication? If so, write out your plan to replace your negative mental tapes with positive ones, define your desired outcomes, plan your approach, and stick with the program no matter what the initial response might be.

C H A P T E R 5

"i" am the "i" in Team

You Count!

Yes, you! Each individual on a team is tremendously important. You can say, "i" am the "i" in team! Your contribution counts. You matter. You affect the outcome of every situation, either positively or negatively.

You impact anyone and everyone in your orbit. For that reason, you have a huge responsibility to your team. The team depends on you to give 100%. If your performance is below average, you'll pull down the team. The team's outcomes depend on your contribution.

We tend to think of teams where we work. Our families are teams, too. And we're part of a much bigger team, our community, which depends on the values and commitments each of us makes. In fact, our society is intricately related with commitments to respect each other, drive in the correct lane, pay our bills, and a myriad of other commitments to each other. Can you imagine going through a day where no one was willing to do his or her part? It would be total chaos!

In each present moment, your attitude and actions are having an impact on someone else. It may be a total stranger or someone who knows you better than you know yourself. You may be completing a transaction with the bank teller or spending time with your significant other. You're always affecting someone else. You can't escape from being part of a team, and your behavior will always affect that team. You may be adding to the chaos without being aware of it!

Picture a speedboat going across a lake. The track of water that trails behind the boat is called the wake. Your personal wake affects every other boat in the water. What's in your wake? The effects can be very negative or very positive.

Our families, friends, and co-workers have to pass through our wake. Do we want to put them in polluted water, or do we want to surround them with a clean, pure environment? Do we want to leave a dangerous and dirty wake for the people we pass on the streets and in our offices, or do we want to leave behind something beneficial? The composition of your wake is your choice.

Think about what you did at work yesterday. Think about what you said to your siblings, your children, or significant other last night or this morning. What kind of wake did you create to start their new day?

How do you treat the team of people you claim to love the most? Do you give them your best time and attention, your energy and insights, or are you so tired when you get home all they get are leftovers? To use a different metaphor . . . do you know those fancy linens and expensive china sitting in the closet? Are you serving your family on the chipped "everyday" stuff and saving the fancy china for "guests"? It is important to treat our #1 team with love, respect, and attention, like they are the people we love and value most in the world.

Three Levels of Teamwork

You don't have any choice about your family of origin team, but you have plenty of choices about virtually every other team you join. Make sure you choose the teams that are right for you. Our relationship with a team is either one of *commitment* or *compliance*, of being in the moment to support each other wholeheartedly, or just filling up space. Don't let your attitude and actions become a hindrance to your family or your team's effectiveness. Unfortunately, plenty of people in homes, families, businesses, and communities are simply in compliance, only doing things because someone else says they *have* to. Make a commitment to be a powerful, positive player.

Compliance is the first level of teamwork. There is no commitment to the good of the team. At least people in the compliance mode aren't actively getting in the way. Sadly, some people aren't even willing to comply with the most basic rules of teamwork. You know them. They're everywhere. You can see several of them at an intersection when their light turns red! These people won't obey simple traffic laws. If the police aren't there to watch them, they do whatever they want without regard for how their choice affects anyone else. How often are we running the red lights at home or at work?

The second level of teamwork is *buy in*, which says, "I understand why we're doing this. I'm not 100% committed, but I understand why." Most people stop at this point. Understanding, it seems, is enough for them. They can have conversations about the outcomes of the family, company, or civic group, but when it comes to volunteering to take responsibility, they don't raise their

hands. Their "buy in" is rational, not volitional.

A few brave souls get to the third level of teamwork—*ownership*. These are the people who give themselves totally to shape the vision, outline the strategy, and implement the plan to accomplish the outcomes that benefit the whole team. Each individual is the "i" in team. Each person owns

> **Everyone on the team has to agree with the vision and make a commitment to play an important part in fulfilling that vision.**

each element of success. The attitude of these people is, "It doesn't matter if anyone is watching. I'm 100% committed to the vision and to doing my part." These people are the heart and soul of any successful team.

For any type of team, achieving the desired outcomes requires a vision statement that states clearly, "This is what we stand for." **Everyone on the team has to agree with the vision and make a commitment to play an important part in fulfilling that vision.**

Rock-Solid Promises

The commitment to take action is the distinguishing trait that separates our rock-solid promises from others' hopeful expectations of us. If you own the vision and the strategy, you make a promise to do your part.

People don't have to wonder what they can expect from you. For instance, when I say I'll take the garbage out on Tuesdays and Thursdays, and I'll mow and edge every Saturday, you can count on that. You don't have to live with hopeful expectations that I will do my part to keep a neat home. I will promise, and that promise is something that can be managed by me and measured by others who trust me to fulfill those promises.

In many families and businesses, misplaced and unfulfilled expectations are a source of tremendous confusion and conflict. We *think* Jim will meet that deadline, but we don't ask him about it until it's too late. We *hope* Mary will pick up the children, but we didn't bother to inform her that she needs to. We *believe* Frank will meet his budget, but nobody gave him the updated numbers. As the old saying goes, "Assumptions make an ass out of you and me!" When we fail to clarify responsibilities and ask people for promises (commitments), we create an environment that breeds misunderstanding and failure. Then we beat each other up over expectations not being met. Most of these issues, though, are surprisingly simple and direct. Aren't most of our arguments at home over things like whose turn it is to clear the dishes and walk the dog?

People blame unfulfilled expectations on the lack

of "common sense." A mother sighs, "Johnny should have the common sense to take out the trash," or a boss explodes, "Mary should have had common sense to get the report done before noon on Friday!"

Blaming others for not using common sense is often an excuse for us not communicating well. It's our responsibility to clarify needs, outcomes, and responsibilities. We can't expect others to read our minds! And here's a news flash: Common sense is not a universal reality! What makes perfect sense to some people is completely foreign to others. We simply must learn to communicate and clarify.

Common sense is what *you* think the world should be, how *you* think people should operate. If someone says, "I love you," it's common sense to say it back, right? Sometimes when someone tells me that I say, "Thank you." That really throws them! But "thank you" is my authentic response in the moment. Isn't that better that a meaningless, rote reaction?

Consider how the myth of common sense affects your teams. You have many expectations based on your version of truth, but if others don't share your perceptions of reality, you probably experience disappointment on a regular basis. As long as you are guided only by your "common sense" instead of shared outcomes and procedures, your team will continue to "let you down."

Clear responsibilities and promises of commitment overcome a lot of wrong assumptions. We've talked about how important it is for each person to have clearly defined outcomes they want to achieve. It's just as important for the whole team to have commonly desired outcomes. If your personal vision doesn't fit with the team's, you and the team will experience conflict, misunderstanding, failure, and undue suffering.

Be a Great Role Model

One of your biggest responsibilities to the team is to be a good role model. We are all role models somewhere, sometime, to some people—like it or not! You're never isolated. **Your actions have a ripple effect, and though you may never see it, the ripples touch lives far beyond your team.** The impact, for good or ill, lasts for a long, long time. In this present moment, you won't know how your example will change someone's day or someone's life. Trust me. I've seen it happen. The smallest actions can have an incredibly powerful impact.

Many people have influenced my life and my work, but two stand out. Philosophically, Dr. Wayne

Dyer's insights and principles have encouraged me to pursue personal responsibility as the key to success in every area of life. His latest book, *The Power of Intention: Learning to Co-create Your World Your Way*, is a wonderful example of his powerful teaching.

The other person who has had a profoundly positive impact on me is Rev. Kirbyjon Caldwell, pastor of Windsor Village United Methodist Church in Houston. Years ago when I worked with Soul Patrol, one of the associate pastors of that church recruited me to develop some creative activities for the youth ministry. I watched Rev. Caldwell lead his staff, shepherd his people, and implement the most creative strategies of any church in the nation. I thought, "There's a man worth following!" In an era when many leaders, secular and sacred, were talking about what God and government should do for us, Rev. Caldwell spoke eloquently about each individual's personal responsibility. He broke the mold. He has incredible insights about people, and he is willing to do all kinds of new ideas to change lives. I've seen other powerful, creative people who seemed to be in it for themselves, but Kirbyjon Caldwell was different. The closer I got to him, the more I was impressed with his integrity.

At Windsor Village United Methodist, I saw

philosophy put on flesh and blood every day. They model what they talk about, and in that environment, I learned a lot! There, I saw first-hand that personal responsibility is the "i" in team. Then, as each individual is responsible and creative, together they experience interdependence. That's when the team really sings!

If you are a parent, you can stop the madness of dysfunction from being passed from generation to generation by letting your children see the positive way to live.

Before I met Rev. Caldwell and his staff and I saw how they taught and modeled personal responsibility, I thought a spaceship had dropped me off on the wrong planet! My concepts of responsibility and right thinking were at odds with all of Western Civilization—and they still are. But there are a few who have insight into what it takes to turn a dream into reality. Those are the people I want to hang around, and that's the kind of impact I want to have on others.

People observe your choices, even when you aren't aware they're watching you. If you are a parent, you can stop the madness of dysfunction from being passed from generation to generation by letting your children see the positive way to live. Let your children learn from watching your constructive, healthy choices.

Too many people are consumed with looking successful, but they experience failure in relationships because their values are in the wrong place. Instead, they need to choose integrity, honesty, love, trust, and tenacity—no matter what. Misplaced values create dysfunction in life that can span generations and destroy companies, families, and individuals.

Your team is counting on you. In fact, it can't be successful without you. The team depends on the special talents that only you can bring to the game. It's your choice to give 100% of what you have to each moment. That's the measure of teamwork. That's the measure of personal integrity. That's the "i" in team.

Most people settle for being mediocre, just getting by doing "good-nuf." When you decide to make the full commitment to yourself and the team, it will be a life-changing experience. **You'll create an amazing environment of trust and confidence—your team will have your back and you'll have theirs.** Just by changing your mind, you will change your world, and theirs, too.

Not Over

Whenever I finish an entry in my journal, I write two words in the bottom right-hand corner: "Not Over."

This notation tells me that as long as I'm alive and breathing, I get to start over again and again. Whatever happened yesterday belongs to yesterday. I can't undo it. It's history.

Today, the score is 0-0. And today, I'm undefeated.

Is today the day you will make a choice to hold nothing back? That choice is yours. Make the choices that determine *if, how,* and *when* things will change. Make these crucial decisions every day. You'll either produce the things you want, or you'll produce the things you don't want. The critical point is to define what you really want, and then go for it with everything you've got!

Change is not a one-time event. You can't think, "I'll make a few changes and be done with it. Then I can go on with my life."

I am a champion of change. I preach it and teach it everywhere I go. I never forget to tell people that change, for all it's benefits, can be terribly difficult. My journals remind me of that sobering fact. I write in my journals every day and keep them close as a reminder. I reflect on the reality of the outcomes that happened yesterday. I made choices. Some worked out; some didn't. I don't beat myself up over the failure and bad decisions because each choice is a chance to learn and grow. Then I move on. I don't spend my life wishing yesterday was different. That kind of thinking wastes energy, and I need all the positive energy I can get for today.

Change is still a process for me. When I'm doing it right, it will always be a process, never a destination. No matter how difficult it gets, the payoff is fantastic! Each day, I'm excited about my choice points. I'm even more excited by the fact that

Each day is an adventure. All decisions are risks, but I'm always ready to take them.

I don't know how each decision will ultimately turn out. Each day is an adventure. **All decisions are risks, and I'm always ready to take them**. I think carefully about the outcomes I want—the ones I cherish and the ones that are secondary. I focus on the ones that mean the most to me, and I make choices all day every day to reach those lofty outcomes. When I stay true to the outcomes I have defined, my choices remain as clear as they can be. I enjoy the moment, each insight, each person, and the result of each choice. I am focused on my life being a compilation of right choices based on my pursuit of the outcomes I'm committed to achieve.

Creating this book was a right choice for me. I'm certain that if you have read this book with an open mind and open heart, you have already started the process of change. Whatever happened in your life until this present moment doesn't prevent you from changing today. It's "not over." In fact, it's never over until you are in the ground. You have the power to make each second of your life matter—even this one.

In my first book, *Change Your Mind—Change Your Word*, I told of an incident in a cemetery when I looked at the headstones and realized that the dash between the dates of birth and death means something very important. It doesn't matter *how long* a person lives. What matters is the *quality* of the life he or she experienced. That's what the dash signifies.

Whatever fills each 24-hour period fills your dash. What will your dash say about you?

Think About This:

1. What "teams" are you on today? Describe the kind of impact, positive and negative, you are having on each one.
2. Describe the characteristics of each level of teamwork:
   —Compliance
   —Buy in
   —Ownership

Which level best identifies your contribution to each team you're on right now?

3. From your experience, what are some examples of how unspoken and unfulfilled expectations have damaged relationships? (Think about your family of origin, your current family, work, friendships, clubs, and church or other house of worship.)

4. What are some current relationships in which expectations need to be clarified and promises made? Describe the benefits in each case.

5. Who has been the most positive role model in your life? Describe that person's impact on you.

6. What are some changes you can make to be a better role model in the lives of the people who are most important to you?

7. How do you respond to the fact that each day is a new day for you, and that no matter what happened yesterday, your life is "not over"?

8. Now that you've finished this book, what are the three most important lessons you've learned from reading it and reflecting on the questions at the end of the chapters?

9. How have these lessons changed your life? How will they change your life in the near future?

10. What are some ways you can help others learn these lessons, too?

About Discover Leadership Training

Discover Leadership Training teaches there is an "i" in team. The "i" stands for independent as well as interdependent. Each person on the team must be a healthy individual before the team can be healthy. Each person systemically effects the team's performance and outcome. They matter . . . they count . . . they always have, and they always will.

An organization's hidden <u>assets</u> are it's <u>people</u>. Empower them to realize their potential, and you'll discover incredible business resources and advantages. When your people become a high-performance team, they will discover their potential more easily. They will also find they have the strength and motivation to go the distance with you.

Discover Leadership Training Programs focus on developing High-Performance Teams by:

- Enhancing the commitment and loyalty among team members,
- Strengthening the team focus on the organizational vision and outcomes,
- Increasing a sense of responsibility and personal ownership of team members,
- Empowering team members to develop new strategies and approaches regarding day-to-day challenges in their roles through hands-on, interactive processes, and
- Specialized corporate training designed to meet each clients specific needs.

Comments by trainees

Here are some comments by people who have experienced Discover Leadership Training:

Tracee Hunt

V.P. of Human Resources, The Philadelphia Coca-Cola Bottling Company:

"I am convinced that I have found a training program that will absolutely be instrumental in the development of the Philadelphia Coca-Cola Bottling

Company (PCCBC) Team...Discover Leadership Training is the most impactful training series that I and many other PCCBC team members have experienced. Here at PCCBC we have sent several managers (with noticeable results) and have a training strategy for 2004 that incorporates Discover Leadership in a major way."

Jerry Ballard

Agency Field Executive, State Farm Insurance

"I have attended a number of good seminars however 'Discover' is not a seminar. It is an experience. Discover truly helps people discover that 'great' person we all have inside. All of my people have had a life changing experience with Discover Leadership Training."

Dennis O'Connell

President, Suburban Auto Body:

"Discover's unique approach to leadership training gave me concepts and tools to effectively motivate and empower my management personnel. By allowing everyone at Suburban Auto Body to participate in the "Discover U experience", I have been able to impart my once single vision and goal of a "World Class Team" to my entire staff. We now understand and look forward to taking our business to the next level as a 'World Class Organization.'"

Jack Pelo

President/CEO, Swire Coca-Cola, USA:

"I personally participated in the training...I felt I gained new insights about myself and how I could become a more effective leader. In summary, I thought the training was very beneficial to our organization. I would strongly recommend it to other companies."

John Greer

V.P. of Human Resources & Development, Smart Financial Credit Union:

"Discover Leadership Training had an immediate and lasting impact on Smart Financial Credit Union's leadership style. They enabled us to make the connection between our heads and hearts, to lead from our heart and manage from our heads."

Contact Discover Leadership Training

"*i* am the "*i*" in team!

DiSCOVER
Leadership Training

To find out how you and your team can benefit from Discover Leadership Training, contact us:

- By phone: 713-807-9902 or 866-22WAYFO (92936)
- By mail:
  Discover Leadership Training
  3525 Sage Road, Suite 606
  Houston, TX 77056-7021
- Online: www.wayfo.com
- E-mail: info@wayfo.com

To Order More Copies of *Hold Nothing Back*

- By phone: 713-807-9902 or 866-22WAYFO (92936)
- By mail:
Discover Leadership Training
3525 Sage Road, Suite 606
Houston, TX 77056-7021
- Online: www.WAYFO.com
- E-mail: info@WAYFO.com